Mrs. Camell

TAKE IT APART
CRUISE SHIP

By Chris Oxlade

Illustrated by Mike Grey

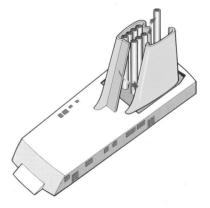

Silver Press
New York

First published in the UK in 1998 by

Belitha Press Limited, London House,
Great Eastern Wharf, Parkgate Road,
London SW11 4NQ

Published in the United States in 1999 by
Silver Press, An Imprint of Macmillan Library
Reference USA, A Division of Prentice-Hall,
Inc., 1633 Broadway, New York, New York
10019

Library of Congress
Cataloging-in-Publication Data
Oxlade, Chris.
    Cruise ship / by Chris Oxlade ; illustrated by Mike
Grey.
       p.   cm. — (Take it apart)
    Originally published in 1998 in London by Belitha
Press under the title: Cruise liner.
    Includes index.
    Summary: Describes the different parts of a cruise
ship and how they work, including the funnels, mast,
bridge, cabins, decks, lifeboats, engines, and hull.
    1. Cruise ships—Juvenile literature. 2. Ocean liners—
Juvenile literature. [1. Cruise ships. 2. Ocean liners.]
I. Grey, Mike, ill. II. Title. III. Series: Oxlade, Chris. Take
it apart.
VM381.095 1999   98-35960
623.8'2432—dc21   CIP
                                AC

Printed in Hong Kong / China

ISBN 0-382-42073-X (LRB)

10 9 8 7 6 5 4 3 2 1

Editor: Claire Edwards
Designer: Guy Callaby
Illustrator: Mike Grey
Researcher: Susie Brooks
Consultants: Elizabeth Atkinson
    and Robin Kerrod

We should like to thank Mulder & Rijke
and Nera Telecommunications for their
help with this book.

Inside This Book

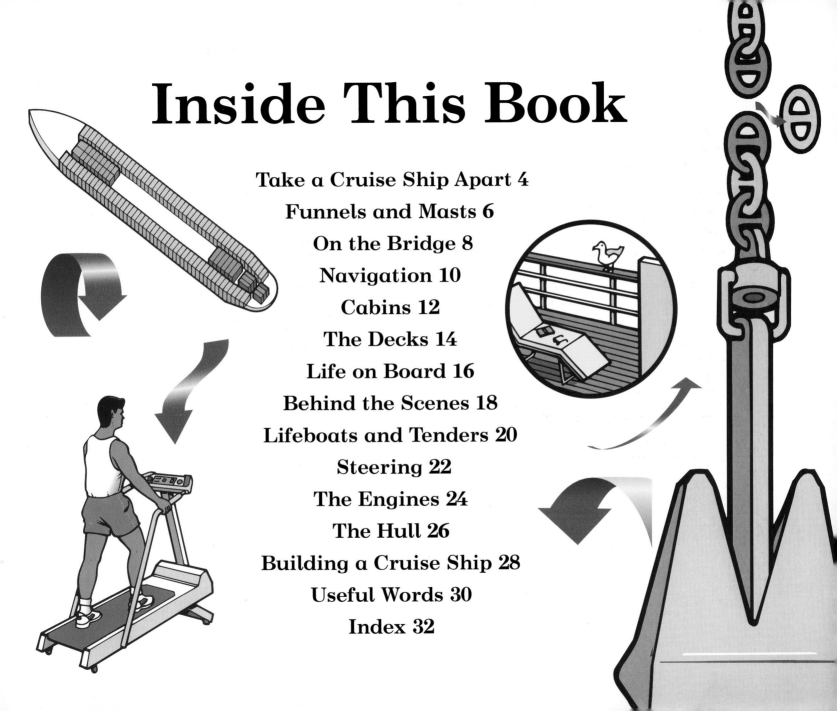

Take a Cruise Ship Apart

☉ A cruise ship is like a huge floating hotel.

◐ A cruise ship has thousands of parts. They are made of metal, plastic, glass, wood, and other special materials.

☽ This book shows you the main parts of a cruise ship and how they fit together.

Stern

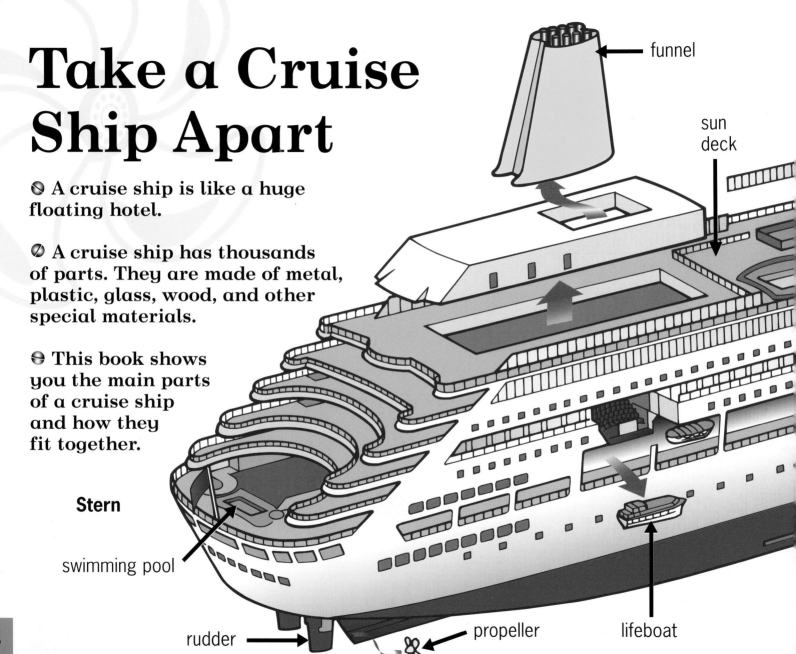

funnel

sun deck

swimming pool

rudder

propeller

lifeboat

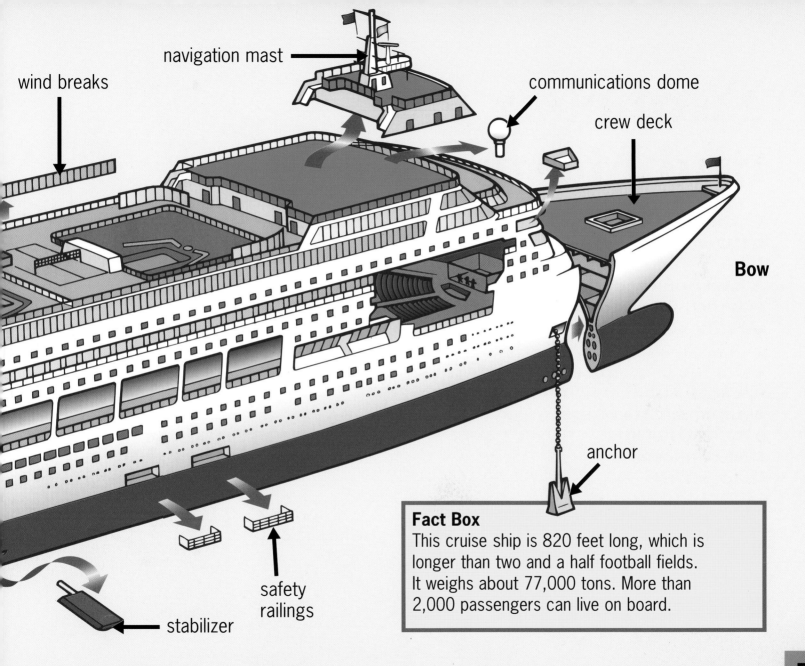

navigation mast

wind breaks

communications dome

crew deck

Bow

anchor

safety railings

stabilizer

Fact Box
This cruise ship is 820 feet long, which is longer than two and a half football fields. It weighs about 77,000 tons. More than 2,000 passengers can live on board.

Funnels and Masts

◉ The funnel and masts are at the top of the ship.

◉ The funnel carries waste, or exhaust, fumes from the engines into the air above the ship.

◉ On the masts there are lights and navigation equipment. There are also instruments that can measure the weather.

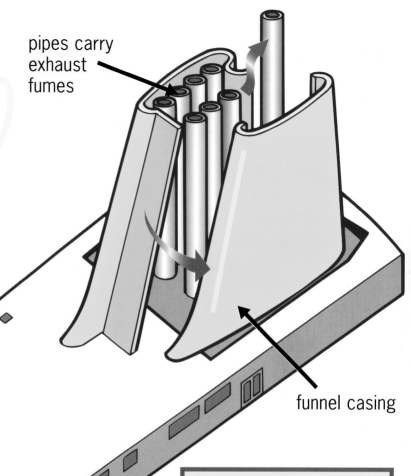

pipes carry exhaust fumes

funnel casing

Fact Box
The first cruise ships in the 1800s had enormous steam engines and needed up to four huge funnels.

Main mast

Lights tell other ships which way the cruise ship is moving, or if it is anchored. The mast of lights is called a Christmas tree. The fog horns are used as a warning to other ships when the weather is foggy.

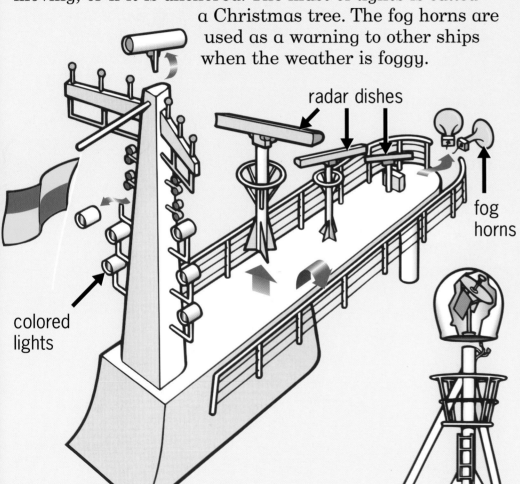

radar dishes

fog horns

colored lights

Lights

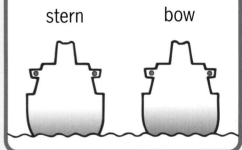

Ships have a green light on the starboard side and a red light on the port side. This means that other ships can tell at night which way the ship is going.

stern   bow

Domes

Inside the domes on the top deck, there are antennas. These send and receive communications signals.

On the Bridge

⊙ The bridge is a room high up at the front of the ship where the crew control the ship.

⊙ The controls for the ship's engines and rudders are in the center of the bridge.

⊙ There is navigation equipment on the bridge and a communications center for talking to the crew in other parts of the ship.

⊙ Plenty of big windows give the crew a good view of the sea ahead.

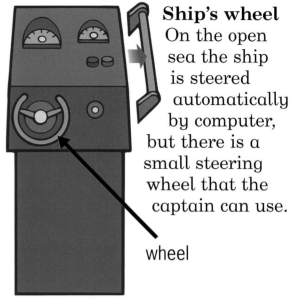

Ship's wheel
On the open sea the ship is steered automatically by computer, but there is a small steering wheel that the captain can use.

wheel

Flying bridge
There is a flying bridge on each side of the ship. Each one has a set of engine and rudder controls like the controls on the bridge.

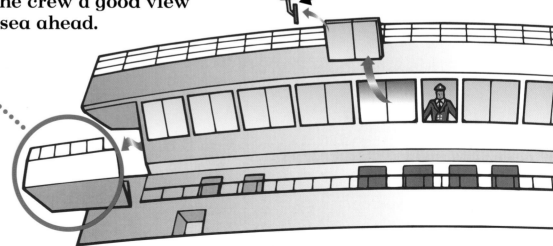

windshield wiper

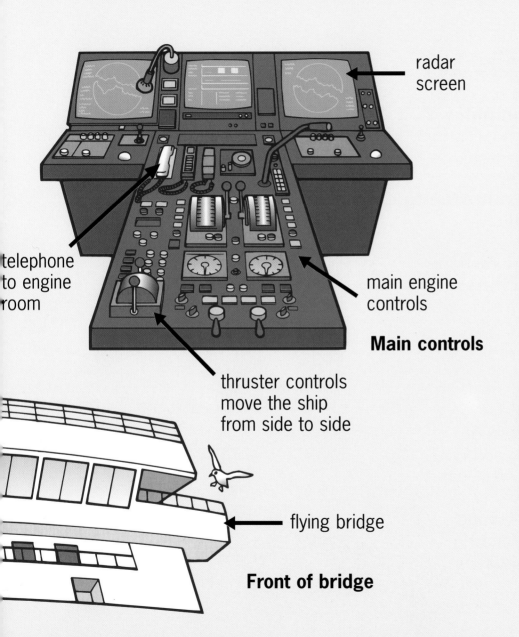

radar
screen

telephone
to engine
room

main engine
controls

Main controls

thruster controls
move the ship
from side to side

flying bridge

Front of bridge

Control panel

The captain has a control panel that overrides all the other controls. He can make the ship speed up or slow down. He can steer the ship forward, backward, and sideways and even turn it around using the joystick.

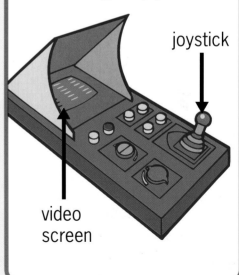

joystick

video
screen

9

Navigation

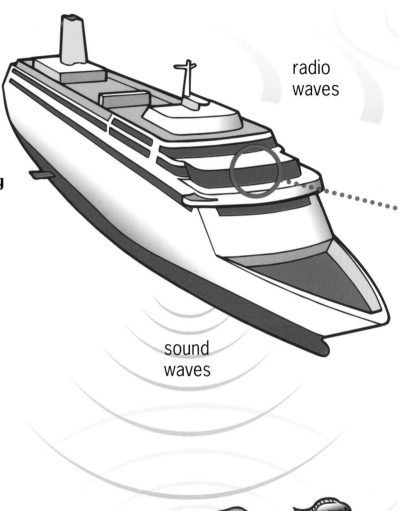

radio waves

sound waves

seabed

- The ship's navigation computer takes in information from satellites and radar and sonar equipment.

- The computer tells the crew exactly where the ship is at any time.

- It also tells the crew how fast the ship is going and in which direction it is traveling.

- The computer can steer the ship automatically.

Fact Box
Distress calls are sent by satellite. This tells rescue services where the ship is.

Sonar
Sonar warns the crew if the sea is too shallow to sail in. It works out how deep the water is by sending out sound waves and measuring how long they take to bounce back.

nearby ship

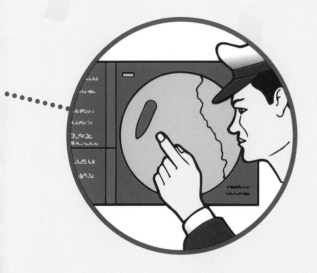

Radar

A radar dish sends out radio waves.
If the waves hit other ships or land, they
bounce back to the dish. The ships or
land are shown on the radar screen.
Radar helps ships to navigate safely
at night and in bad weather.

navigation satellites

Ships use signals from
space satellites to help them
navigate. A receiver picks
up signals from a number of
satellites in different parts of
the sky. It can then work out
the ship's position accurately,
to within a few feet.

satellite antenna

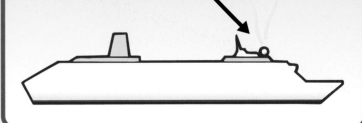

Cabins

⊘ The passengers sleep in cabins on the upper decks of the ship.

⊖ Each cabin is like a hotel room. It has beds, closets, a dresser, and a small bathroom.

⊘ Some cabins have a balcony and lounge area as well.

⊘ There are also cabins for the crew.

Fact Box
In the future some cruise ships may have apartments instead of cabins. People will be able to buy an apartment and live on board.

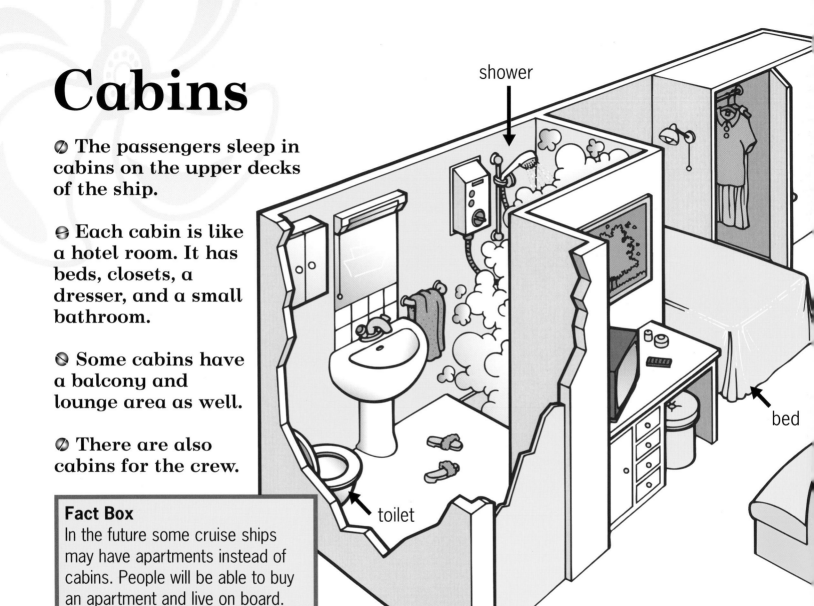

shower

toilet

bed

12

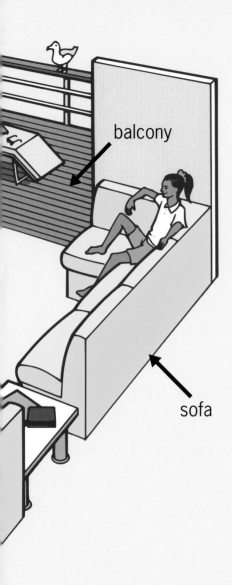

balcony

sofa

Fitting in the cabins

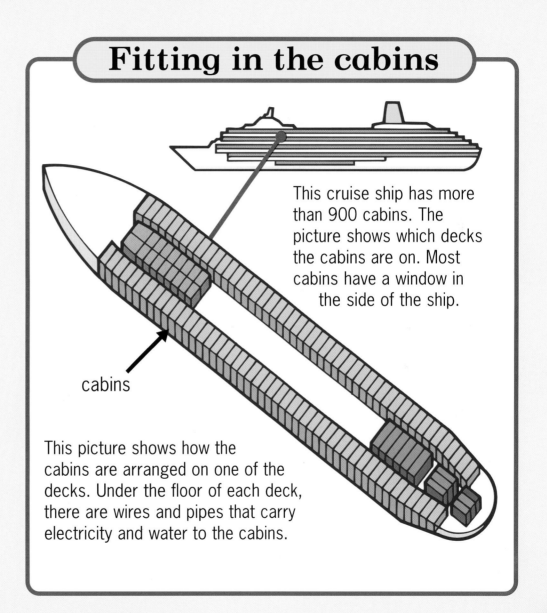

This cruise ship has more than 900 cabins. The picture shows which decks the cabins are on. Most cabins have a window in the side of the ship.

cabins

This picture shows how the cabins are arranged on one of the decks. Under the floor of each deck, there are wires and pipes that carry electricity and water to the cabins.

The Decks

⊙ A ship is divided up into many decks, one above the other. The top deck of the ship is called the sun deck.

⊙ The passenger decks are made of wooden planks laid side by side over a metal frame. Staircases lead from one deck to another. Large cruise ships also have elevators.

⊙ Large glass panels stop the wind but let the sunshine through.

⊙ The crew have their own sun deck with a swimming pool and tennis court.

Fact Box
There are 5,200 fire and smoke detectors around the ship. They are fitted in every cabin, storeroom, and storage locker on board.

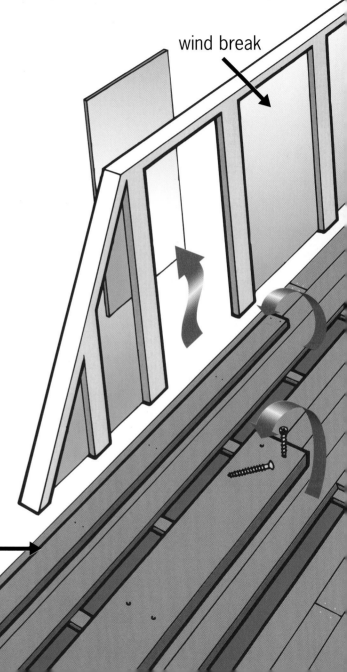

wind break

deck plank

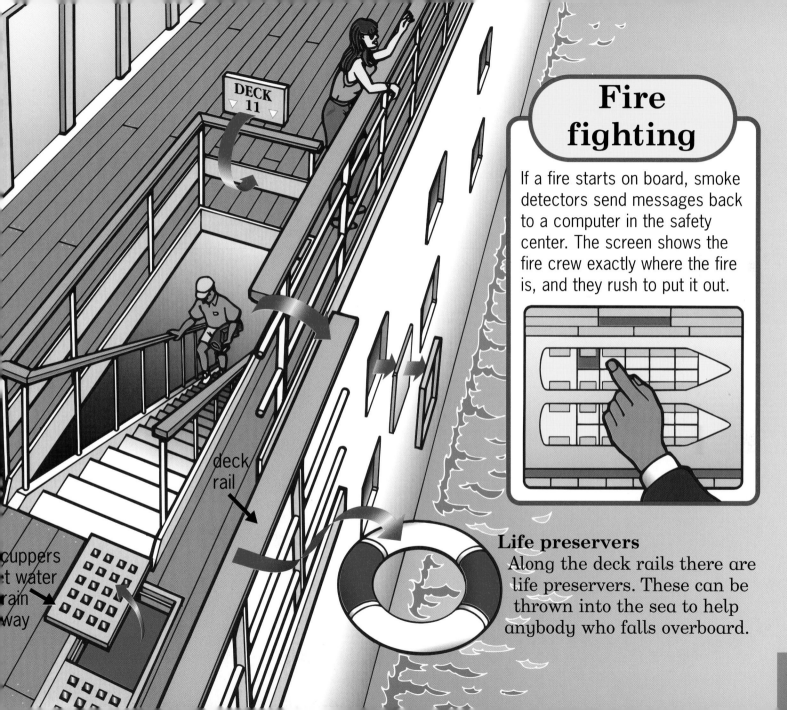

DECK
11

deck
rail

cuppers
water
drain
way

Fire fighting

If a fire starts on board, smoke detectors send messages back to a computer in the safety center. The screen shows the fire crew exactly where the fire is, and they rush to put it out.

Life preservers
Along the deck rails there are life preservers. These can be thrown into the sea to help anybody who falls overboard.

Life on Board

⊘ There are lots of activities and entertainments for the passengers on a cruise ship.

◑ On the sun deck there are deck games, swimming pools, and areas for sunbathing.

⊘ Inside the ship there are cafes, restaurants, a gym, a library, and even a large theater.

Deck games
On the sun deck there is a mini tennis court where passengers play a game like volleyball using small hoops.

Jacuzzi

lights

filter

Swimming pools
There are several heated pools on the sun deck. Underneath the deck is machinery for heating and cleaning the pool water.

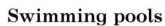

Meals
Passengers can eat in restaurants inside the ship or out on deck. Between them they use thousands of tables, chairs, knives, forks, spoons, cups, plates, and dishes.

Gymnasium
There is no room to go running to keep fit on the ship, so there is a gym filled with exercise equipment.

Entertainment
In the evenings the passengers can watch shows and movies in the ship's theater. It has the most up-to-date lighting and sound systems, and even a revolving stage.

Behind the Scenes

◉ **There are many parts of the ship that the passengers never see.**

◉ **These are mostly on the lower decks, often below water level.**

◉ **There are many storerooms for supplies and storage tanks for water and fuel.**

Laundry

The ship's laundry has huge washing machines, dryers, and pressers. They can wash, dry, and iron 3,500 sheets every day. A long chute carries dirty bedding and clothes from the upper decks down to the laundry.

metal grid

Galley

The ship's huge kitchen is called the galley. The stoves have special metal grids to keep hot pans from tipping over in rough weather. There is also a bakery for making bread and cakes.

Waste disposal

Garbage goes to the waste disposal center where it is burned, broken up, or crushed. Any metal cans are recycled.

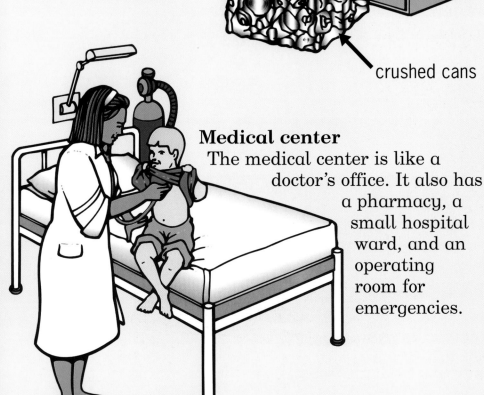

crushed cans

Medical center

The medical center is like a doctor's office. It also has a pharmacy, a small hospital ward, and an operating room for emergencies.

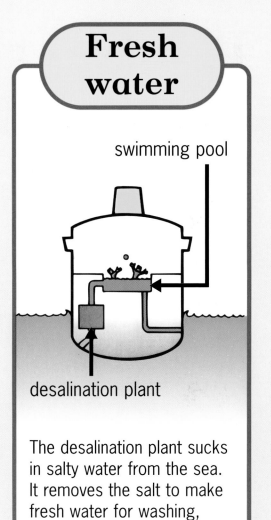

Fresh water

swimming pool

desalination plant

The desalination plant sucks in salty water from the sea. It removes the salt to make fresh water for washing, cooking, and filling the swimming pools.

Lifeboats and Tenders

⊘ The ship carries lots of emergency equipment in case it catches fire or begins to sink.

⊘ The large lifeboats can carry up to 150 passengers each.

⊘ There are enough life jackets for everybody on board the ship.

⊘ The equipment is brightly colored to make it easy for rescuers to see.

Fact Box
Lifeboats and tenders are driven by small diesel engines. Each one carries food, water, a first-aid kit, and flares.

Inflatable rafts
There are life rafts as well as lifeboats. They inflate automatically in an emergency.

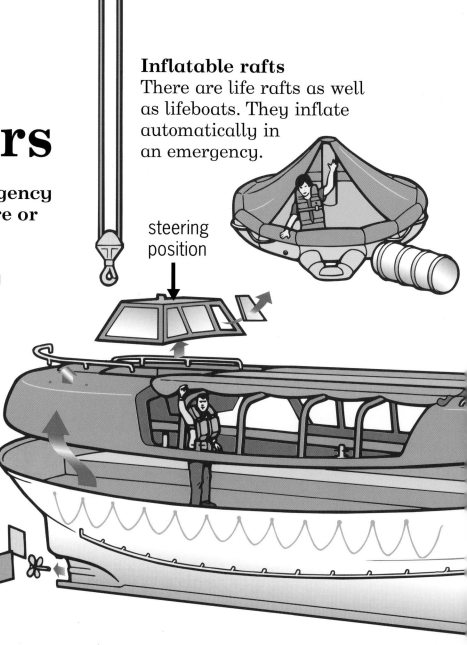

steering position

Lowering the lifeboats

1 The lifeboats are stored high on the side of the ship.
2 The boats slide out from the side of the ship on davits.
3 The boats are lowered for the passengers to climb in.
4 The loaded boats are lowered into the water.

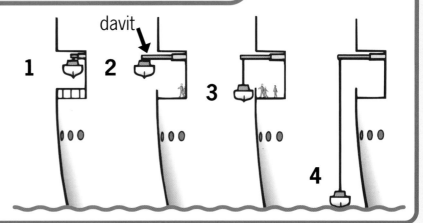

davit

1   2   3   4

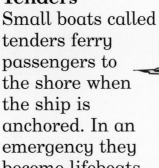

← pulley attachment

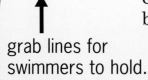

grab lines for swimmers to hold.

Tenders
Small boats called tenders ferry passengers to the shore when the ship is anchored. In an emergency they become lifeboats.

Steering

◑ There are two large rudders at the stern of the ship. They turn from side to side to steer the ship.

◑ There are also four thrusters that move the ship sideways.

◑ Stabilizers keep the ship from rolling from side to side in rough seas. This helps to stop passengers from feeling seasick.

Fact Box
A ship must be well balanced. As supplies and fuel are used up, sea water is taken on board to help balance the weight in the ship.

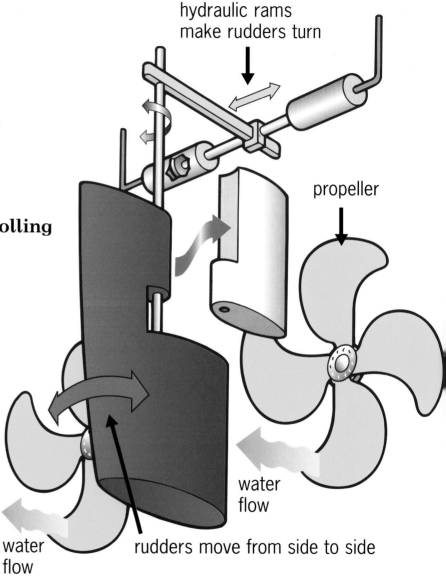

hydraulic rams make rudders turn

propeller

water flow

water flow

rudders move from side to side

Thrusters

Thrusters push water through tubes in the hull. They can make the ship move to one side or the other, or turn on the spot. Thrusters are fixed at the ship's bow and stern.

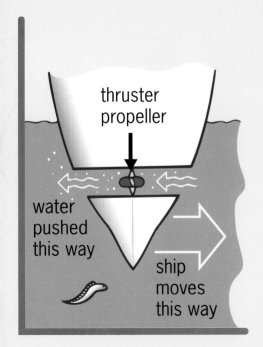

thruster propeller

water pushed this way

ship moves this way

Stabilizers

The stabilizers are like fins that fold out from each side of the hull.

If the ship rolls to one side, the stabilizers move to make it roll back upright.

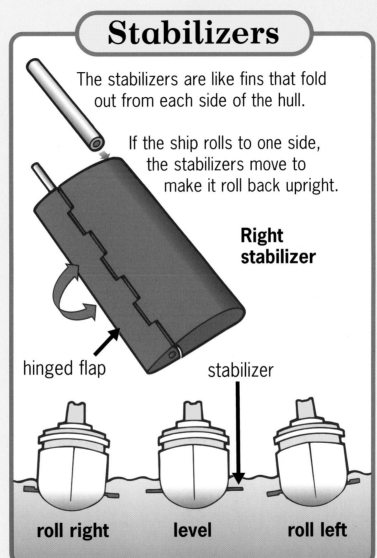

Right stabilizer

hinged flap

stabilizer

roll right　　**level**　　**roll left**

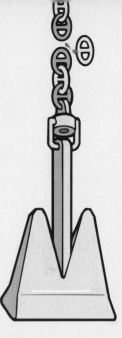

Anchors

If a ship needs to stop when it is not near a dock, it has to lower its anchor. The anchor digs into the seabed and keeps the ship from drifting away.

The Engines

🔩 This cruise ship has eight huge diesel engines. Each engine is as big as a small bus.

🔩 The engines are in the engine room. The engine room takes up the bottom three decks at the stern of the ship.

🔩 Some engines drive the propellers that move the ship along.

🔩 Some engines run generators that make electricity for the lights and electrical machinery on the ship.

Fact Box
Each electricity generator could make enough electricity for a town of 40,000 people.

Bridge controls
The speed and direction of the ship are normally controlled by the officers on the bridge.

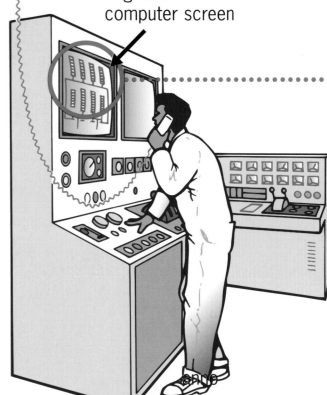

engine control computer screen

Engine controls
Next to the engine room is the engine control room. Here the ship's engineers check to see that the engines are working properly, using computer screens.

Engines for power
Four six-cylinder engines turn electricity generators that make electricity for the ship.

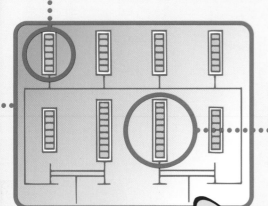

Propellers
Four of the engines turn the ship's two propellers. Between the engines and propellers, there are gear boxes. The gears slow and control the propeller speed.

gear box

propeller shaft
propeller blade

Main engine

Each engine has nine cylinders with a piston in each one. The pistons turn the propeller shaft. Here's what happens when the engine is working.

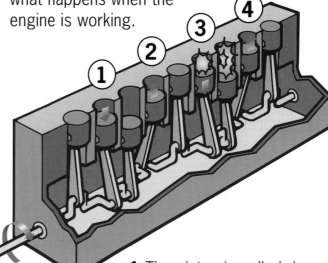

1 The piston is pulled down, sucking air into the cylinder.
2 The piston moves back up, squeezing the air and making it very hot. **3** Fuel is squirted into the hot air and explodes, pushing the piston down. **4** The piston moves up, pushing the burned fuel out of the cylinder.

The Hull

🔩 The outer body of a ship is called the hull. It is like a huge metal box.

🔩 The hull is made up of a strong metal frame covered in metal sheets to make it watertight.

🔩 Inside the hull are metal floors called decks and metal walls called bulkheads.

Deck strength

The decks are made from sheets of metal with metal ribs underneath. The ribs keep the deck from sagging.

Fact box
The hull is painted with special paint that keeps barnacles from clinging to it.

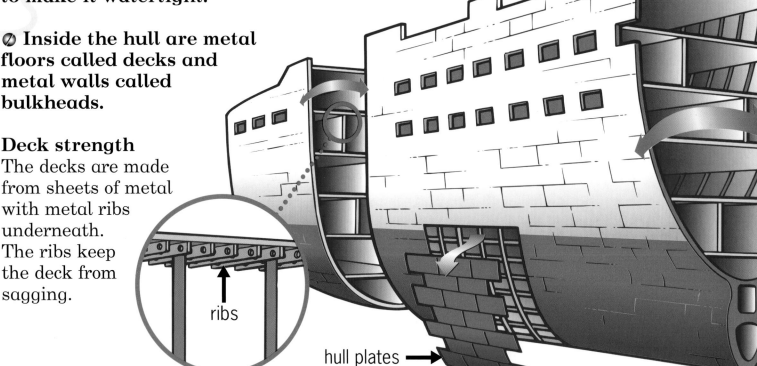

deck

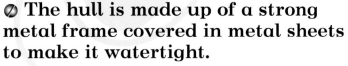

ribs

hull plates

26

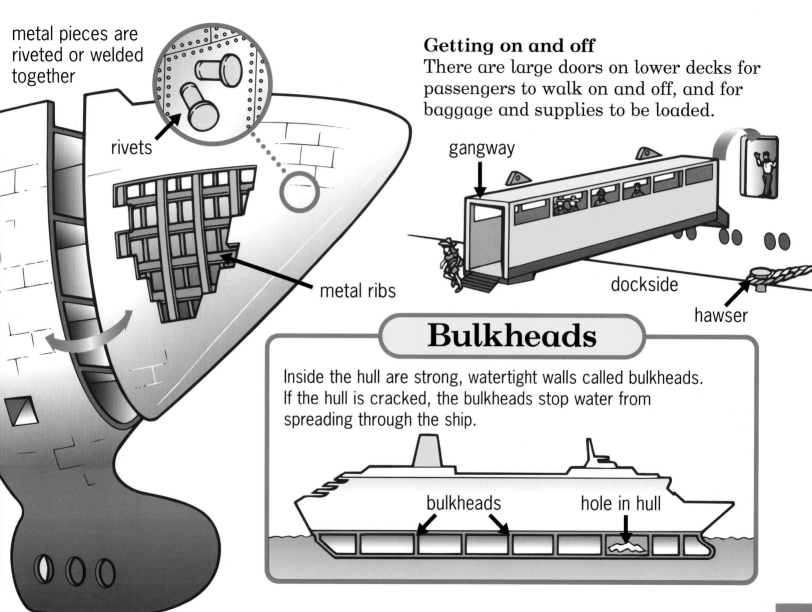

metal pieces are riveted or welded together

rivets

metal ribs

Getting on and off

There are large doors on lower decks for passengers to walk on and off, and for baggage and supplies to be loaded.

gangway

dockside

hawser

Bulkheads

Inside the hull are strong, watertight walls called bulkheads. If the hull is cracked, the bulkheads stop water from spreading through the ship.

bulkheads

hole in hull

Building a Cruise Ship

🔘 Modern cruise ships are built in a dry dock inside an enormous shed at a ship-building yard next to a river.

🔘 Sections of the ship are made outside the shed and joined together inside.

🔘 Thousands of workers help to make the complete ship, from steel workers to carpet fitters and electricians.

Fact Box
When a ship is finished, it goes on sea trials to check that everything is working properly.

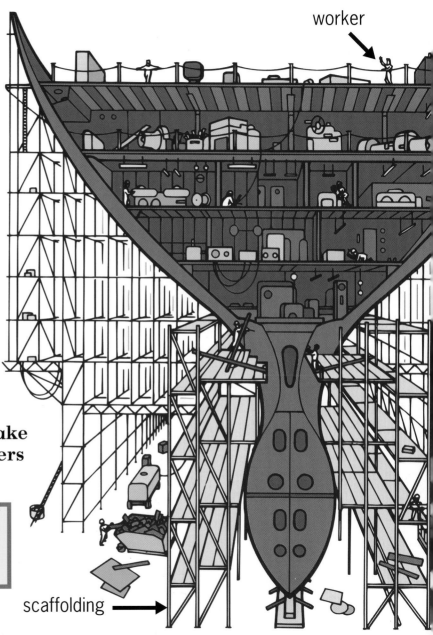

worker

scaffolding

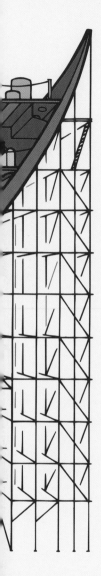

Floating out

When the hull and decks are complete, the dry dock is filled with water, and the ship is floated out. The ship is then finished. This is called fitting out.

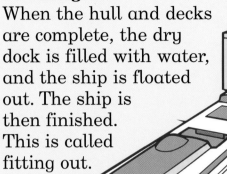

dry dock

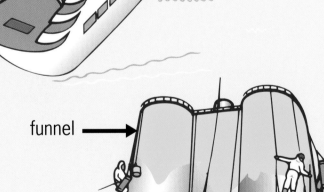

funnel

To make sure that a ship will work properly in all kinds of weather, designers often build a model of the ship and test it in a huge tank of water.

Shipshape

Just like a car, a ship must be regularly checked. Every few years a cruise ship also has a refit. The outside is repainted, new engines may be fitted, and inside parts, such as carpets and furniture, may be replaced.

Useful Words

bow The front of a ship.

crew The people who work on a ship.

cylinder A tube in the engine where fuel burns.

davit A type of crane that lowers lifeboats into the sea.

deck The name for a level or floor in a ship.

desalination Removing salt from sea water.

diesel engine A type of engine that burns diesel fuel. Burning the fuel moves pistons in cylinders, which makes a shaft spin around.

dock A closed-off stretch of water in which ships can be moored or repaired.

dry dock A dock from which the water can be removed.

flare Something that sends out a blaze of light to tell people that help is needed.

fuel A liquid burned inside an engine to make the engine work.

gears A set of wheels with teeth around the rims. When two wheels are placed rim to rim, one wheel turns the other. They help to control speed.

generator A machine that makes electricity when its shaft (a round rod) turns.

hawser A thick rope that is used to tie a boat to land.

hydraulic ram A special kind of cylinder. Oil is forced into the cylinder to make the piston inside move in or out, which controls other machinery, such as a ship's rudder.

inflate Fill with air.

joystick A small stick that moves backward and forward and from side to side. It is used to control a machine.

life jacket A jacket that fills with air to keep a person afloat in the water.

navigation Plotting a route and following it.

piston A piece of metal that moves up and down inside the cylinder of an engine. On a ship this turns the propeller shaft, which makes the ship move.

port The left-hand side of a ship.

propeller A set of large blades that turn around.

propeller shaft A rod that turns the propeller.

radar An electronic apparatus that uses radio waves to detect objects and stormy weather.

ribs Metal rods that strengthen a ship's hull.

rivets Metal fasteners used to join pieces of metal.

rudder A flap fixed to a ship's stern that turns from side to side to steer the ship.

satellite A craft that travels around Earth. Satellites collect information and send it back to Earth by radio signals. They also transmit telephone calls and television pictures.

scaffolding A frame that is used to support workers and materials when something is being built or repaired.

shaft A round rod.

sonar An apparatus that can detect objects under water. It works like radar, but uses sound waves rather than radio waves.

starboard The right-hand side of a ship.

stern The back of a ship.

weld To join pieces of metal by melting them together.

Index